PANDEMIC PRATER: PASTEL PALLIATIVES

GENARO J. PÉREZ

PANDEMIC PRATER: PASTEL PALLIATIVES

iUniverse books may be ordered through booksellers or by contacting:

iUniverse
1663 Liberty Drive
Bloomington, IN 47403
www.iuniverse.com
844-349-9409

ISBN: 978-1-6632-1542-0 (sc)
ISBN: 978-1-6632-1543-7 (e)

Print information available on the last page.

iUniverse rev. date: 01/07/2021

Table of Contents

ECHOES

Listen to my words submerged within these pages

Unknown reader in our pandemic penumbra.

Are you nobody too?

I am Steppenwolf

A stranger in a strange land

Happily secluded in my cave

Away from people whom I scorn

Their pettifoggery and malevolence

shall make them sweat and whine about their condition.

My voice is hoping to reach those I do not see

I do not ask who you are, that is not important to me

Read my words as a form of penance

And enter the door I am unlocking.

PANDEMIC PRATER: PASTEL PALLIATIVES

HUMAN VOICES

Paltered voices come and go

"listen to me dear bro:

You must kiss ass

Before you can kick ass,

Go to their parties,

Intermingle and fuse,

it is easy to make it

by just doing so."

To my dismay I cringe and fake it.

I drink their wine and follow their chatter

The air we share is small and dry

Talking of trivial things make me scatter

From these coarse people clutching their gods.

PANDEMIC PRATER: PASTEL PALLIATIVES

MASK POLITICS

All my neighbors call me to task

For being so different and wearing a mask

Since covid arrived am secluded in my cave

To do otherwise would be so depraved

Thousands have passed for not wearing a mask

Bats with baby faces appear at night

I look out the window and don't see my neighbors

Am I the last one alive?

PANDEMIC PRATER: PASTEL PALLIATIVES

AFTERNOON DELIGHT

She was so much delight—the widow next door

After covid's arrival I kept her away

I was a frightened kitten she wanted to pet

I bolted my doorway and remained indoors

Our afternoons in bed came to a halt

Her sweet panocha I feared to savor

And her ruby nipples I dreaded to suckle

because COVID-19 is not little flu.

When the ambulance took her away

To my dismay—I never saw her again.

COVID-19

How long will you visit US

Unwelcome stranger

Whom everyone wants to avoid

It lurks everywhere and is nowhere

I fear a cup of coffee at Starbucks

And buying my groceries at United.

The shapes of the 145,000 casualties arise!

The crowds of the mask less

portend future corpses

Oh what horrible mess!

They don't believe in science

Since their book doesn't buy it:

Darwin's theory will soon befall.

PANDEMIC PRATER: PASTEL PALLIATIVES

PANDEMIC PORTRAIT

Who's that old man

that looking glass displays

Who scowls at me as if inspecting

A stranger in my own home

his long head of hair suggesting

A caricature from wizards' flicks

And the prominent silver beard

A portrait of old King Lear.

He reeks of stale garlic

his eyes are encircled by

unknown countries' flags:

(yellow green blue red violet)

such presence is quite a drag!

MASKLESS FREEDOM

I want to be free

It is in the constitution

It is my nature to be free

despite the consequences

I would rather die free maskless

than forced to cover my face

give me liberty or give me death.

I don't care about the story

Of the scorpion and the frog:

Where the scorpion asked the frog

To carry him across the river

cruising on her velvety back.

The frog promptly refuses

voicing her safety fears

The brute scorpion assures her

he would never dare sting her:

"I treasure my life too much!".

So the frog foolishly agrees

Hops into the winding currents

She often frolicking crossed

Piggybacking her is the feared arachnid.

Midway down the river

treacherous scorpion stung the frog.

She admonishes him

With a painful whimper

"Foolish scorpion we'll now succumb."

The scoundrel gurgled profuse regrets:

"such is the consequence my nature begets."

PANDEMIC PRATER: PASTEL PALLIATIVES

PANDEMIC REVERIE

OOO Alice, sweet Alice

You come through the looking glass

Into my nighttime pandemic trances

Like a succubus from opium hallucinations.

Intermittently appearing as student in my classes

donning a Japanese students' uniform

A short dark-striped dress over your knees

Your titillating legs agape granting me a yoniscape

Oh such fragrant heavenly gate

With a hint of fuzz crowning your puss.

Would I were a cunning linguist

With a gift of tongues to delineate

Your myriad of heavenly charms.

Following your vicious laughter

I could hear a whisper from your lips:

"Verás, pero no comerás"

Mercilessly responding to my ogling

Looking at me with your deep hazel-blue eyes

Ooo, no painter could do them justice!

OO Alice, sweet Alice, with flower rosy lips

And such flowing blazing red tresses

Your coy cajoleries drench my dreams

I dream/cream for thee sweet Alice

I am mystified by your girlish mystery.

Am I a blasted bleating blatant

bloaten blooming idiot to you?

When you said "Mare Nostrum"

Were you foreboding a rendezvous

In Barcelona, Sardinia, Sicily?

Perhaps our rollicking into the waters

Of wetted life?

There I vision you, sweet Alice,

in unapparelled naturalness.

PANDEMIC PRATER: PASTEL PALLIATIVES

JESUS IS MY VACCINE

Predicants with zigzaggery delivery

With stale words preaching

Affirm that Covid is not to be feared

And that masks are the manifestations

Of the unholy beast soon to appear

Jesus is the giver of all good things

Christ will never allow you to stumble

He'll never fall asleep on you

Wearing a mask means you have tumbled

Become a doubter of our beloved Jesus

The lord of the seven days

We should be in dependence of Christ

Let us become mask-less

holy-troopers of Jesus.

Amen, Nema, Mena, Eman, Mean, Maen.

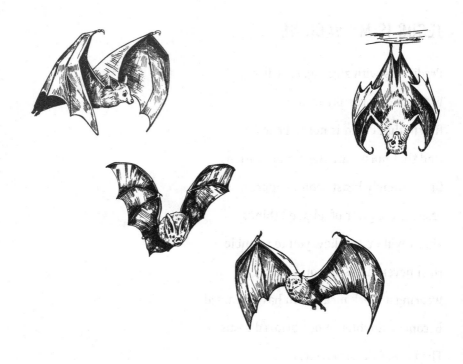

PANDEMIC PRATER: PASTEL PALLIATIVES

COVID PARTY

Omega Omega Omega

cordially invites you

To our first annual Covid party!

Dedicated to the king of viruses

His majesty Corona of the novel

Royal family of bats.

We respectfully request you bestow

$30.00 at the door which will go

Into an account which will be

Given to the fortunate invitee

Who develops little flu.

PANDEMIC PRATER: PASTEL PALLIATIVES

MY THREE PUSSYCATS

I am spending these pandemic months

With three lovely cats:

Harliequeen, Bruja, and Lola.

They have different personalities these three

And I think I know why that is.

Bruja is the oldest and wisest of the three

She was brought to me with Calico Mama

By Midnight one winter evening

Midnight was the girlfriend of an old friend

Of mine of twenty years, Blue Boy was his name

Midnight came looking for him

and could not find him

for Blue Boy had passed days earlier

so she brought these stray females

who were pursued by five alley Toms

I rescued Bruja and took her to the vet

The calico cat escaped and got pregnant

She came back one cold March evening

Very pregnant and about to give light

And she had her seven kittens in my garage

Calico Mama had three boys and four girls

I gave away the three tommies

Humans tend to prefer males to females

I kept Lola, Maskat, Harliequeen, Tearie,

And Calico Mama who looked after her girls.

We were all a happy family

Until Calico Mama and Maskat went away

Scouting the mysteries of the alleyways

Teary appeared dead at my patio's doorway

Blood pouring from her mouth

From some unknown wallop

Perhaps from a catphobic neighbor

I am left with Bruja the oldest

And the wisest tortoise shell cat

I have ever had living with me

She is a peeper and speaks in tongues

When I awaken at night

I meet her *tapetum lucidum* in the dark

Inspecting me and she also gazes

When I read and compute;

Frequently while she sleeps

I hear her talking in strange languages

I never considered studying.

Lola looks like a pinto horse

White with calico patches

With a streak of podofilia

Always licking my toes

Perhaps thinking it is

limburger cheese ready to devour

with tiny love-bites that tickle.

Harley is a true calico

With scaredy-cat personality

And a melodramatic perspective of life,

She is also into frotage,

Not to be confused with fromage,

Although food is her thing

She is twice the size of the other two

The Vet told me runts usually have

That sort of problem since they had

To struggle for their mother's teat.

My three female felines

Provide my pandemic days

With wonderful distractions

And the days, weeks, and months

So swiftly pass and are

filled with unending satisfaction.

PANDEMIC PRATER: PASTEL PALLIATIVES

SWEET MARY ISVATA

Where have you gone my pandemic paramour?

Your departure was feared from the start

when this corona virus tore the world apart.

Your fragrance has infused my house

And you are here wherever I go

As I pace like a caged tiger

looking at my cave's walls

Covered with posters and paintings

Thinking of Michael Angelo

And reading the DECAMERON.

While life outside my house goes on and on!

DREAMING WITH YOU

I had a dream with putty cat last night

I gave my wife of thirty-three years

That pet name because of her softly purring

When we made love all those years

Until dementia took her away

And her love for me became hate

Believing I conspired with nurses to kill her.

We were attending a conference

In a third world country in a city

With poorly paved streets

Filled with people who gawked at us

As we walked holding hands.

Their stare was of curiosity about strangers

Not the malignant scrutiny at MLA meetings

Those pelucid minds that inhabit the lobbies

Those professionally piqued professors.

Not a glance was given

To some of those old professors

lodging at the conference's hotel

Who staggered with a walking stick

wobbling down the meetings and corridors

holding hands with young undergraduates.

In the waking dream we arrived at a *Mercado*

Bursting with colorful petite shops

And the moon shone in an haze of colors

Where a myriad of curious items

Were displayed hanging from the walls

There was a multicolored blanket

With a calico cat framed at the center

She pointed to the bedspread and said:

"I want it!"—and she was gone.

I woke up in a world slowly decaying

About to be exterminated by corona virus.

PANDEMIC PRATER: PASTEL PALLIATIVES

TEMPUS LOQUENDI ET TEMPUS TACENDI

The stars became wandering holes

in an unfamiliar sky that has no future

we are in a waking nightmare

a vain emptiness chockfull

with the dark hawk of bats

the trees melted in the air and

the bamboos speak as if weeping

The year of our Lord 2020

Or more precisely 17-VIII-2020 AD

During pandemic times when

21,720,713 humans have been infected

And 776,157 have died planet-wide

From COVID-19 and in the USA

5,408,208 have been infected and

170,131 have died from Little Flu.

Words have lost their significance

This is a time when falsehoods

Trump truthfulness

A time when liberty is cankered

With simulation

A time when fear renders men

Stupid and miserable

A time when sciolism/religion

trump science

A time when creationism

trumps evolution

A time when honor

Is a mere fragment of virtue

A time when free elections

Will be taken away.

Friends, Americans, countrymen

Lend me your eyes

I write these lines during Democracy's

Burial ceremony in remembrance

Of what we were

Not to praise it

QAnon and el general trompeta

Has told you that the Union was corrupt

Filled with ambitious men

A deep state trying to overtake

the government of the chosen one

a swamp that needed draining

and el general trompeta

and QAnon are honorable men

my heart is in the coffin with Democracy

and pray that it will survive Covid-19

why have American lost their reason?

Is it the result of pompous rituals

Theatrical ceremonies

Used to delude and terrify?

Has el general trumpeta convinced

So many with his magical moments?

We must not forget that el general

trompeta is an honorable man

and he will make the USA

a better country where the selected

will survive this plague

sent by the Almighty

el generalísimo's imposing figure

seems to have been propelled

from a Botero painting.

Will he be declared president

For life like his admired master and

(can we use that word?) puppeteer

El puto de Putin?

Would that we could take out

everyone of them g.d.m.f. trumperos c.s.

Fascists all of them—as Pound

Sommo Poeta would proclaim

Today when bats are hawking

And a regime is based on grand

Larceny—silver beaks in the night.

When the constitution is in jeopardy

And gun sales lead to more gun sales

A country in which the sun is

Going down precipitously:

We shall oscillate like a pendulum for

Tromperos don't care about the constitution.

Will we ever be untrumpeted?

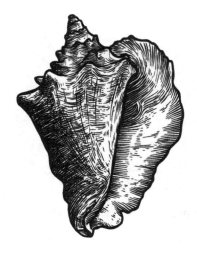

PANDEMIC PRATER: PASTEL PALLIATIVES

COITU INLUMINATIO

I have drawn endless verse portraits

Of Juana, Juanita mi amiguita,

With wormest venerection

Denouncing my continuing devilries

I have been frequently inebriated

Drinking from your furry cup

My mind drifts like weed in the

West Texas wind thinking of

Your crotch like a young sapling

With the scent of sea breezes:

A nest softer than cunnus—

I always wondered why Saint Paul

Was so very hard on fornication!

I will always be an eater of grape pulp.

PANDEMIC PRATER: PASTEL PALLIATIVES

GAS LIGHTING

It was a bright cold day in March,

and the clocks were striking thirteen

COVID-19 stroke furiously

But Big Brother told us

It would go away in the summer heat

Like magic—his gut told him so!

Beware of the fake news

Their language corrupts the truth

general trompeta warned us all

and He kept telling us that

in our beautiful USA existed

alternate facts—what you heard

was not the truth—only He preserved it

Don't forget:

The USA is a great family and

el general trompeta is our big brother!

COITO ERGO SUM

Remember that Tallinn tea room?

When we chattered about Emily

And I said: rowing in Eden

Ahh the sea, were I to moor

Tonight in thee

And you intoned:

Inebriated of air am I!

You disputed my feelings:

No hay amor sin celos

Saying that it was a macho statement:

Considering the female as property.

Oooo! Those were our days ...

Your penelopean patience

And I the professionally piqued professor.

Where are they now?

You were the ant and I was the grasshopper

Always tipping the velvet.

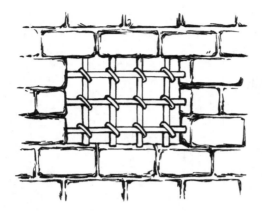

PANDEMIC PRATER: PASTEL PALLIATIVES

CAGED CHILDREN

Immigrants, legal/illegal represent

One of the gravest dangers to USA.

The caravan approaching last year

Is a case in point.

Therefore, quote Mr. Miller, we

Must find a way to inhibit them

From invading the USA, USA, USA

And soiling our great nation.

If we take away their children

If we rip them away from their parents

These unwanted invaders

Will understand borders better.

And so it goes that children

Were separated from families

And placed in pens

And developed serious

Psychological problems

Molested and tortured

And died from COVID-19

The flu, and other

childhood ailments—

niños sin barquitos,

niños sin ositos,

niños sin juguetes.

Luna, luna, dame pan

Que tus hijos no me dan

Sings a little girl

In the middle of the night.

PANDEMIC PRATER: PASTEL PALLIATIVES

LIKE LEMMING . . .

The gop (grand obdurate party) is marching

Precipitously into historical oblivion

Following their beloved Duce

El generalísimo trompeta

Who will make USA great again

No one will take their white privilege

& there is nothing they

Will not do to retain their status

Covid's deaths are acceptable casualties

After all, they are occurring

Among minorities and the aged.

Excess population demands

Slaughter at intervals—

slow motion purgative

that will make USA pure & strong

the boot-lickers bellow

the best

is yet

to come!

PANDEMIC PRATER: PASTEL PALLIATIVES

UNLAWFUL LAW ENFORCERS

I read an article in the *Atlantic*

March, 1969—a bloody year

There were some studies

Showing the presence

Of repressed criminal behavior

Of some police officers—

SNCC is gone

SDS gone too

MLK is gone

John Lewis is gone

Police brutality is still here!

Law-enforcers

are not screened psychologically

their behavior has become iniquitous

the police deliberately encourage violence

they provoke violence to make arrests

lying too has become a part of the procedure

they abuse a man and then arrest him

they shoot a man and then arrest him

a man who defies the police is punished/killed

such situation feeds the impulse to riot

with video cams every where

they can't slip & slide

and try to hide

like they did before.

Pray for these law-enforcers

For they have no principles—

Quote a black father:

I tell my sons that when they

Have encounters with the cops

They should do whatever

they are commanded,

Disregard any insults or blows

Any abuse is endurable—

I rather see them with bruises,

Physical & psychological

Than having to go to the morgue

To identify them—

Sad—so sad, so very sad

Triste—muy triste

Bonjour tristesse

TRISTISSIMUS

печальный

λυπημένος

B L M

PANDEMIC PRATER: PASTEL PALLIATIVES

VORTICIST PICTURE SHOW

When I have migraines

(I stopped having them in my twenties

Now they are back:

trompeta took office)

When I close my eyes

I see vorticist paintings:

Black and white lines

& multicolored triangles.

Yet, I can't forget trumpeta

Our dear leader

The defiler against race—

The core of evil.

The canker corrupting all Things—

Hydra entering all things—

Truth, we beseech thee

Clarity, we beseech thee.

Creators, wherefore are thou CREATORS

Now that we need you so

Help us overcome the darkness

That is about to overwhelm

Our beloved country!

Only NESHEK

Is legated?

PANDEMIC PRATER: PASTEL PALLIATIVES

ANOTHER LOVE POEM TO MY WIFE

M'amour, m'amour,

Where are you?

Where have you gone

Come to me in my dreams

I beg you—

I lost my center

When you departed

It seems so long ago

You took that long/eternal

Journey without return.

Winter will be here soon

But the snow will no longer

Be like sea foam

樂趣

Happiness left my life

Very long ago.

!Ay, amor

Que se fué y no vuelve!

PANDEMIC PRATER: PASTEL PALLIATIVES

JUANITA ISABELITA PLURABELA

When I awake after dreaming

With you

I feel the vain emptiness

That virgins must feel

Upon returning to their homes

You showed me Lubbock's pleasures

Of life that weren't to be found

Anywhere else in this cursed planet.

Until you left me forever

There were no stinking afternoons

When the wind was blowing from

LBB east where the stock yards are

The carrion sniffers in the faculty

Did not exist—

Perhaps they were hiding away

Fearing your power &

your righteousness

& your incisive intellect

That so easily sliced & diced

Frauds, sexists, and misogynists.

That foolish and malignant

Rumanian dwarf, I remember,

Was a vivid illustration:

El enano maligno

(Of childhood fairy tales)

Like many in our profession

Unfortunately—

Pícaros everywhere

Sent papers to professional meetings

To be listed on the programs and

Never performed—their CV's claimed

Otherwise—hoaxers them all.

El enano epitomized that breed &

Juanita swiftly exposed him:

He wanted one of his friends

To be hired for a French position

rather than a Female

who had superior qualifications—

Juanita voiced her opinion to the Dean

Thus the female was hired

& the tenured dwarf was fired.

PANDEMIC PRATER: PASTEL PALLIATIVES

CREATOR(S) WHY HAVE YOU LEFT US

¿Señor(es) porqué nos abandonaste?

lama sabachthani?

ut quid me dereliquisti?

You left your seed in this forsaken planet

And then left after discovering

That your experiment had gone defective

You left us imperfect and malignant

Covetous, greedy, lustful,

Inheritors of the deadly seven:

Why have you create humans so imperfect?

Why do sinners' ways prosper?

Was it a flaw in the experiment

you failed to amend?

Are you so imperfect that your

Only solution is to flee

Like a frightened rabbit?

Pro bono malum

The horror of it!

PANDEMIC PRATER: PASTEL PALLIATIVES

MASS MAN I

I will never see

That light of greatness

(wise men talk about)

Not even Eliot's flicker

Down here

In the Dungeon

Where we all gather

To reject "constructive dissatisfaction":

It usually led to unhappiness

And the anguish of the weak.

THIRTY THREE

We counted the years by the numbers

Of regional, national and international conferences

The number of pages written for the monograph in progress

The cities, the people, the colleagues, the papers

All forgotten: the excellent with the bad and the mediocre.

Gourmet delights blended with somber bodegas

With sawdust and oyster shells

Concealing ancient wooden floors.

I still have them all with me:

Obsolete files waiting to be erased

To give room to vulgar experiences

That precipitates the interminable question:

Is this all there is?

PANDEMIC PRATER: PASTEL PALLIATIVES

MASS MAN II

The horror of it
I am starting to be content
Content to be nobody
To be nobody too!
I will not be besieged
At professional conferences
and boring book readings
by groupies calling me:
Maestro, Maestro
Wanting to shake my hand
to tell me about the novels
they are writing and
plot summaries galore.
No more, no more.

PANDEMIC PRATER: PASTEL PALLIATIVES

FADED SEPIA

I am beginning to disremember your face

Waking-up without you is now normal.

There are no longer drums beating in the morning

With the wake-up service we frequently expected.

Your side of the bed is now cold and scentless—

That natural fragrance your body radiated

Is becoming just another remembrance.

Corona has taken over my life

Outside everything is filled with strife.

PANDEMIC PRATER: PASTEL PALLIATIVES

DELICIOUSLY INSANE

Oh! how deliciously are the notions

That you are again here with me

Whispering ideas together with

Erotic sweet nothings

Reminding me why my obsession

For you and everything coupled to you.

A mistake was made and your passing

Was prematurely reported!

Oh! Will insanity bring you back?

RAINING IN LUBBOCK

Dirty melted crystal drip and
Drop dulling the night into sleep
I remember you in those cold
Winter nights when our bodies
Seeped warmth from each other
And you purred like a kitten
Cuddling me into sleep.

PANDEMIC PRATER: PASTEL PALLIATIVES

FOUL CREATURES

I see their deplorable dear leader

With a large foul paunch

& the yellowish-red face

& his bleached blonde hair—

I hear the disinformation

He is incessantly launching—

Would that we could

Find a winged horse

Riding knight

Who shall do

A brave and noble deed

With a blade of metal sharp

And a very keen way to strike

That obese yellow fiend

Whose power is so mighty—

And his witless foul followers

white-power much starved

They must disturb the system

& erect that repulsive wall

Plunking our country into turmoil.

Let's hope his days of power

Will soon end & pass

Before our country into

Smoke and loathsome filth is cast.

& the foul deplorable minions

Power-hungry much starved

In smoke eternal shall dwell

For submitting to the whims

To one monstrous autarch

Who mocks and cast aspersions

On our veteran heroes

Who were wounded and pass on

Defending our freedom—

No redemption should ever

Trompeteros attain

from hades everlasting where

they must forever dwell.

Dilexisti malitiam super benignitatem

PANDEMIC PRATER: PASTEL PALLIATIVES

DIVINE MADNESS

Where O where are you my bella

I need you now, Fair Mistress

Love of my life

Enflame some inspiration

Let my finger tips

Spin out the words

Like the three fatal sisters

Spin humans' fates

One's threads of life

I want to recreate you,

portray the love for my angel baby—

you were an angel of the heavenly guard

For whom my heart still burns

The one I mourn every morning:

Every day and night on these keys

In vain I knock a chain of words

For many, I fear, it will all be

No more than meaningless mock.

PANDEMIC PRATER: PASTEL PALLIATIVES

188,942

Have passed to date, 7-X-2020

On this the third year and ten months

Of trompeta's malignant domination

There is little to celebrate

And much to commiserate

The dear ruler is very cruel

In deed and discourse to countless

His proclamation of herd immunity

Meant sacrificing the old with impunity

The morgues are overflowing

with COVID-19 cases every morning

men of wit, women of courage, are there

many important figures, giants of the theatre

WWII and Viet Nam veterans

Poets, sports figures, actors,

grandfathers & grandmothers,

have prematurely passed

It is all the responsibility

of an incompetent president

elected by a misguided minority

who thought that a confidence-man

—a sham blonde figure—

was the One they long awaited

that fearless leader

an American der Führer

who would make contraception

and abortion illegal

& plonk black & brown people

Back where they belong

& build a high lily-white wall

That will return the USA

the way the country used to be:

make the USA great again.

PANDEMIC PRATER: PASTEL PALLIATIVES

BOLERO I

More than five years have passed

Since you left me one day in May

And my life is now in disarray.

Profound pain caused your departure

because you were the gleaming star

that shone above all others

and guided my life through pleasure

& all its painful displeasures:

bounteous bloody tearing tears I have shed

all these years thinking of you:

I hope that as my heart grows older

It will react to your memory much colder.

IS MY SORROW YOUR ECSTASY?

With a wicked smile she said "silence"

And my heart shot blood into my face

I was curious about her research—

A group of us surrounded her

During a professional conference

At L.S.U. in Baton Rouge

Her being an eminent scholar

The subject made sense

For the small talk I tried to start

The rouge of her lips I craved to taste

So I named several authors

Who use silence in some of their works.

Quote Genaro: you are reading

Tristram Shandy and *Tres tristes tigres*,

I presume, and some of the novels

Of Juan Goytisolo.

My response struck the subject

& we immediately connected

a few years later

she became my wife

and for thirty-three years

the woman of my life.

NEVERMORE

In my dark & silent bedroom
Very late into last night
My ceiling fan flung a shadow
Of a bird of prey in flight
A dark rising shade
with prodigious wings expanded
the image floated over me
as I rested frozen with fear—
I was waiting for Morfea
To whisk away immediately
my wholly consuming plight
reminiscing of things past
Morfea arrived without my noticing
& gave me a dream with my departed wife
she was driving some unfamiliar
& strange vehicle
Her hair was yellow like ripe corn—
As my despair and fear swelled
I asked her when she was returning
She replied: NEVERMORE.

PANDEMIC PRATER: PASTEL PALLIATIVES

TEMA D'INFAMIA

Truth has died from one thousand cuts

As we arrive to Vico's fourth stage

We are rapidly entering the age

When the USA shall fall:

Alarms sound here, there, everywhere

Chaos reigns supreme

with COVID-19:

Trompeteros blindly believe

The virus is a hoax.

Mother Nature is avenging

Humans insensitive abuse

She is employing effectively

A very deadly blitzkrieg:

Corona all over the country

overwhelming wildfires in the West

& multiple hurricanes in the East—

Aiding her in such endeavors

Are the trompeteros

Who have catapulted the gop

Into trompeta's pop cult

Trompeta's meta is

to become an autocrat—

twelve more years,

twelve more years,

don't you know:

The Dragon is moaning

The Tiger is screaming

The Bald Eagle is crying

There is no honesty remaining.

Can we justify God's way to man?

This is an embittered hour

When we in our COVID bubbles

Are moping melancholy mad

And don't know where to turn

Do we wish we had Astolfo's horn?

Can all this continue to be so bad?

USA, my beloved USA, have you gone mad?

The adoration of a mad man

By the easily duped trompeteros

Are killing the USA—

The USA is dying, the earth is dying

Does that mean anything to you?

Are you one of them too?

PANDEMIC PRATER: PASTEL PALLIATIVES

HERD MENTALITY

Generalísimo trompeta is the ideal

Freudian subject because of his spiel

He projects and tongue-slips a great deal

His minions are demonically captured

By a conman who has them enraptured

Within a world where gas light

Is used as a matter of course

Trompeta's attention span is worse

Than a child's game of *rayuela*

He has no shame and he's very dishonest

The senate gop is his staunchest devotee

He said he could kill a man on 5th Avenue

Without repercussions and he's not cuckoo

He has killed 300,000 to date and his feat

We all fear is not complete.

Are we to become the United Banana States?

PANDEMIC PRATER: PASTEL PALLIATIVES

ZOOMING

I teach online all my classes

And stay indoors away from the masses

My maskless maddening neighbors

Whose front porches are crammed

With signs exhorting the reelection

And the very long continuation

Of their beloved leader's protection

From the presumed extinction

Of the privileged Aryan race

And so the days move along

Creeping like a green lizard on my porch

Going from zoom class to zoom class

Absenteeism increases as COVID

Makes the rounds like beer and tequila

In our university bars and frat houses

It is becoming more difficult to communicate

They know so very little about history

They never heard about our super president

FDR and his amazing works program

That took us out of the depression

And his fire side chats during WWII

They know nothing about geography

And about literature not even a clue

T.S. Eliot, Hemingway, Faulkner

are all unknown and so is Wagner

I played for them the "Magic Flute"

And they believe I am just cuckoo.

The female students do practice an art

Most make-up artists in Hollywood

Would find it smart:

Eye brows like Garbo and Crawford

Multicolored finger nails like flowers

Lips with colors that rainbows covet

Toenails that suggest wild strawberries

What should I do to gain their attention?

Just move on and proceed with the lessons?

PANDEMIC PRATER: PASTEL PALLIATIVES

RBG: SUPER JUSTICE

A woman for all seasons has passed:

You will not hear a priest declare it during mass

Neither will a Christian TV-pastor preach it

Nor an Imaam in a Mosque will declare it

Thanks to RBG my wife

The love of my life shattered

the glass ceiling & flattened the Ivory wall

an eminent Hispanist who was considered

inferior to her fellow male professors—

equal treatment laws bestowed her

the just equality she deserved,

even though she was superior intellectually

to most male professors at her university.

The encounters with male professors she experienced

Deserve to be told to all women in academe

Thus they will learn and recognize extreme misogyny

RBG: gigante intellectual: *Requiesce in pace*

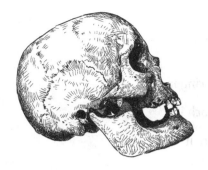

SWEET BIRD OF YOUTH

Youth my divine treasure where

Oh, where have you gone

Every year that passes, for you I mourn

Fleeting youth that brought so much delectation

I can't remember those almond eyes without exaltation

The Long Beach of 1959 and you are still with me

Sand around our colorful beach towels

Wet sand clinging to your strawberry toenails

Your scent I sometimes inhale in many public places

Where is she and all the other beauties I once knew

Some in the biblical sense and others just fleetingly

We had so many places to go and so many things to see.

Where is my curly black head of hair

With the duck tail and the pompadour

That girls liked to caress so affectionately?

Like wakes in the sea these remembrances

Will disappear into infinite nothingness.

PANDEMIC PRATER: PASTEL PALLIATIVES

ACADEMIC DEMONS

La meretrice invidia strolls academic corridors

Spewing slanders and deception

To fervent listeners eager to gather rumors

About their academically superior colleagues

There is no hyper-democracy in academe

Rank demands privileges and recognition

Los de abajo begrudge such cast system

So they are ready to bring them down

Anyway they can from their position

Those who can't publish instruct undergraduates

Those who don't publish and can't teach

Become administrators and torment

for revenge and amusement

C'est la guerre in academe!

PANDEMIC PRATER: PASTEL PALLIATIVES

BOLERO II

Another evening in my cave

Hibernating like a bear, fearing COVID

And by evoking you I become a slave

To all our moments during all our explorations

Tutti li miei penser parlan d'Amore.

Knowing I will never see you again

Becomes so difficult to explain

To myself like this plague annihilating

So many seniors who had so much life.

Are humans soon to become extinct

Like dodo birds and white rhinos?

Oh how I wish you were right

And there is something beyond

This corrupt and decadent realm.

Abbandonate ogni speranza voi

Che entrate qui.

PANDEMIC PRATER: PASTEL PALLIATIVES

SAN SEBASTIAN

Ora pro nobis San Sebastian

Ora pro nobis patron of pandemics

Liberate us from the mortal virus

Keep us from having Neanderthal genes

With all the consequences that it means.

My green back yard has developed sun spots

And my beautiful pistachio tree is dying

How could I possibly be devastated

By such unimportant petty issues?

San Sebastian liberate us from this crown of thorns

Remove from us esta corona de espinas so unjust

San Sebastian provide us the elixir to deconstruct

This Virus from some unknown netherworld

No woman, no man should be doomed and hurled

Into the pits of pain, agony, and gnashing of teeth.

Is lethargy part of our punishment as well?

SONG TO MY PANDEMIC SELF

Here I sit and while away hour after hour

O Mother Nature you brought Corona to flower

To punish human's hubris and cruelty.

Is this an enchanted atmosphere?

Is this my lovesick dream for penance?

Why do you allow the church to take

ill-gotten goods without stomach ache?

I am cooped up among these heaps of books

Coated with the everlasting West Texas dust

Cough and cry from allergies I must

Since reading and writing is all I am allowed

By your Corona sentence I am enshroud.

No odor of grace emits from my armpits

A whiff of my garlic inebriates my cats

Mother O Mother why have you spread

this vengeful curse of the market bats.

PANDEMIC PRATER: PASTEL PALLIATIVES

PANDEMICS ARE SHORT, ART IS LONG

I need to know now what I don't know
What I know fulfills very few needs
All these musings need some explanation
This Pandemic make us believe in incantations
Wild dreams fill my mind with wonder
People I know and people I knew enter
And exit with very little explanation
Long lost relatives make the dream-scene
With very strange and forgotten conversations.
Television displays long lines of the food insecure
And reports of bodies piling up in the morgues
All those tragic events are Covid's devastation:
Trompeta talks about a forthcoming vaccination
And is pressuring scientists for a hasty cure
Corruption is ubiquitous under trompeta's rule
Like termites feasting on rotten wood
Tromperos are demolishing USA's morals
Everything these days is so obscure.

PANDEMIC PRATER: PASTEL PALLIATIVES

CANCIÓN

The days follow one another

Like a chain gang tripping along

Hoping for their sentence to be over:

In my cave I daydream with Gong

Li waiting for the vaccination & leave

This confinement and sling in Singapore

to see the most beautiful woman in the world.

Is that too much to ask?

I want to see the roaring sea dancing on the beach

And the blue moon swaying before howling dogs

And the silvery stars trembling like lovers waiting

And the palm trees coupling with the blond sand.

Covid, Covid go away

And don't you comeback another day!

PANDEMIC PRATER: PASTEL PALLIATIVES

DEAD BABY BALLAD

Poor Baby Doe

Her body was found

A few years ago

In Boston's rocky shore.

A tiny toddler

Inside a bundle:

A black plastic bag

  Strong for heavy duty:

   packing a zebra blanket and baby clothes.

Those were her escorts

During that woeful crossing:

A journey without return.

Today it was revealed

Bella was her name.

Oh depraved mother:

  Your demon seer lover

   delivered numerous blows

to Bella's tummy

he meant to exorcise

those demons

that kept her from sleeping.

Did you fear the imps

Under your crib,

Baby Bella?

Those heartless inhumans

So very wicked

May they be perpetually condemned:

quivi le strida, il compianto, il lamento.

PANDEMIC PRATER: PASTEL PALLIATIVES

TROMPETA SUPREMO

I see traces of Rodríguez de Francia

In trompeta's private and public demeanor

Although without genetic relation the fever

For absolutism is visible in his malacia.

Are we in peril from the proud white boys

& QAnon to mention a few of his storm troopers?

Will these fringe groups be the annihilators

Of USA's democracy so admired in the world?

May all be hurled into bottomless perdition:

Such place Eternal Justice has prepared.

PANDEMIC PRATER: PASTEL PALLIATIVES

PANDEMIC PENANCE

I hope you have enjoyed these pandemic musings

Dear reader, as we navigate in the same cruise ship

These waters so filled with pain & tribulation.

We sail on the river Styx and so often we hear squeaking

bats and rustling cries and lethargy is overwhelming us.

I hear the moaning of ambulances outside my house:

Other humans have succumbed to the virus

Will there be an end to all this madness and suffering?

Will there be a Hollywood Ending

Where Evil will be punished and the good rewarded?

December 4 of the Pandemic year 2020

ABOUT THE AUTHOR

Genaro J. Pérez has a B.A. in English and Spanish from Louisiana State University in Baton Rouge, and an M.A. and Ph.D. from Tulane University. He is Professor of Hispanic Literature at Texas Tech University. His primary scholarly interest is Twentieth and Twenty-First Centuries Spanish and Latin American literature as well as Chicano literature. His academic publications include: *Formalist Elements in the Novels of Juan Goytisolo; La novelística de J. Leyva; La novela como burla/juego: siete experimentos novelescos de Gonzalo Torrente Ballester; La narrativa de Concha Alós: Texto, pretexto y contexto; Ortodoxia y heterodoxia de la novela policiaca hispana: Variaciones sobre el género negro; Rabelais, Bajtin, y formalismo en la narrativa de Sergio Pitol; Subversión y de(s)construcción de subgéneros en la narrativa de Rosa Montero.* His books of poems include: *Prosapoemas; Spanish Quarter Notes; French Quarter Cantos; Ten Lepers and Other Poems: Exorcising Academic Demons;* and *Estelas en la mar: Cantos sentimentales.* His narrative includes: *The Memoirs of John Conde* and *French Quarter Tales.* He is Co-Editor and Co-Publisher of *Monographic Review/Revista monográfica* (Volumes I-XXVIII); and is Co-Editor of the journal *Dura.*

ACKNOWLEDGEMENT

I want to thank my daughter, Nicole T. Pérez, for the design of this book.

www.nicoleperez.net